# God is a Wonder!

Bedside inspirations to nourish your **spirit**

# Gwendolyn Hayes

Published, September 2019

Printed in the United States of America

Library of Congress Cataloging in Publication Data

ISBN: 9781728927107

Hayes, Gwendolyn

God is a wonder: Bedside inspirations to nourish your spirit

Photo, Cover Design & Artwork: Gwendolyn Hayes

Keywords: Christian hope, comfort, encouragement, prayer

*To: my sister Dorothy,*
*who inspired herself as she healed.*
*Your encouragement to others is contagious!*

*To: my sister Brenda,*
*for your faith, scripture life, and dedication to family.*

*To: my great nieces, Adora, Alisa, and Charnice,*
*and daughter, Gwendolyn II,*
*for your gifts of caregiving.*

# Your sun is coming!

*Open thou mine eyes, that I may behold*

*wondrous things out of your law. (Psalm 119:18)*

*Arise, shine, for your light has come, and the glory of the Lord rises upon you. (Isaiah 60:1)*

God is divine. There is no other as amazing as He is.

He is all knowing, and He loves you.

He is the God of hope and love.

He is the God of grace and mercy.

And He loves you.

Stay encouraged by seeking His wonder.

**Gifted to:**

CHERIE McCLAIN

**Date:**

SPRING 2020

**From:**

DENEASE MOORE

**God** is a wonder!

God **is** a wonder!

God is **a** wonder!

God is a **wonder!**

# God is a wonder!

## CONTENTS

Introductory Prayer to our God of Wonder

## <u>INTRODUCTORY PRAYER TO OUR GOD OF WONDER</u>

*Dear Heavenly Father, Creator of all. God of Wonder, I thank you for just being you, Lord. You ARE a wonder! You are glorious, you are generous, and you are gracious to each of us every day. Your blessings are endless, and your grace and mercy are so undeserving. But yet, you give us your love every day. I praise you, Lord. You are so faithful to listen. It's your name, oh, that Name, that we exalt above all others. No one or no 'thing' is more worthy. I pray that this tiny book blesses and nourishes the receiver, because it is inspired by your wonderful Word. Let the receiver know that relationship with you is EVERYTHING! Touch their lives and their journeys, Lord. Please hold them close in their long days and their nights that may seem endless. Teach them the art of encouraging themselves with your Word. Give them rest that only the God of Wonder can supply. Until you come, may we be comforted, nourished and equipped through your Word. I do give all the glory to you.*

*In the wonderful and matchless name of Jesus the Christ, Amen.*

# God is a Wonder!

## *Wonder in His Word*

### A bedside thought

Growing up in the Baptist church, the pastor would often tell us, "If you live long enough, you're gonna have some valleys so low you may think you have lost your mind. If you live long enough, you're gonna have some mountains so high you may have put your mind on not making it over." No matter what circumstances are in your path, God is with you. Right now. Right where you are. Keep His Word close to your heart. Rest well knowing God will hold you close to His heart. It is so good to have Him as your friend.

If I tried to recite all your wonderful deeds,
I would never come
to the end of them.

Psalms 40:5

I will praise the Lord
no matter what happens.
I will constantly speak of
his glories and grace.

Psalm 34:1-7

He is your praise and he is your God,
the one who has done mighty miracles
you yourselves have seen.

Deuteronomy 10:21

And now, brothers,
as I close this letter
let me say this one more thing:
Fix your thoughts on what is true
and good and right. Think about things
that are pure and lovely, and dwell on the fine,
good things in others. Think about
all you can praise God for and be glad about it.

Philippians 4:8

14

### A bedside thought

You know, sometimes you start praying and you drift back into your troubles and come back and drift back out. But think about it. You still know who the Father is. So, you need a bit more time with Him. It's okay, you've got something started. God wants us to take time to remember Who He is. Take your time. He is patient. He knows your thoughts even when you can't speak. It's okay. The God of Wonder hears you.

Block out the traffic of the world and meditate on His word.

Then I lay down and slept in peace
and woke up safely,
for the Lord was watching over me.

Psalm 3:5

He has sent me to heal the brokenhearted
and to announce that captives shall be released, and the
blind shall see.

Luke 4:18

Anyone
who calls upon the name of the Lord will be saved.

Romans 10:13

'Because of your little faith,'
Jesus told them.
For if you had faith even as small as a tiny mustard
seed, you could say to this mountain, 'Move!' And it
would go far away.
Nothing would be impossible.

Matthew 17:20

### A bedside thought

Soak yourself in the memories of what God has done for you already. Celebrate what He has done for your brothers and your sisters, too! Our Holy Father's right hand holds yesterday, today and tomorrow! Hold to God's unchanging hand. God's right hand still represents power, authority, and sovereignty! Now rest.

You are not alone.
He saw no one was helping you,
and wondered that no one intervened.
Therefore, he himself stepped in to save you through his
mighty power and justice.

Isaiah 59:16

You will keep him in perfect peace,
whose mind is stayed on You,
because he trusts in You.

Isaiah 26:3

Be anxious for nothing,
but in everything by prayer and supplication,
with thanksgiving,
let your requests be made known to God;
and the peace of God
which surpasses all understanding,
will guard your hearts and minds
through Christ Jesus.

Philippians 4:6-7

Christ is our source of wonder.
Jesus is the way, the truth and the life.
No one comes to the Father
except through me.

John 14:6

24

### A bedside thought

Even when you are afraid, you have a security system in God. All you have to do is, remember Who you belong to. Remember Who has *your back*.

His love is stronger than your fear. Now rest.

When you lie down,
you will not be afraid,
when you lie down,
your sleep will be sweet.

Proverbs 3:24

Return to your rest, my soul,
for the Lord had been good to you.

Psalm 116:7

Peace I leave with you,
My peace I give unto you:
not as the world giveth, give I unto you.
Let not your heart be troubled,
neither let it be afraid.

John 14:27

These things I have spoken to you,
that in Me you may have peace.
In the world you will have tribulation;
but be of good cheer,
I have overcome the world.

John 16:33

### A bedside thought

We are so messed up, so we need to hurry up and get to Jesus and let Him know that we are telling everybody that we've got the latest, earth-shaking, news that - He is good all the time and all the time He is good! The GOOD BOOK says Let EVERYTHING that has breath, praise the Lord! How can we stop praising Him? His greatness is ENDLESS! No End! So, we are in such perfect harmony when we are praising our Lord.

A time to cry and a time to laugh.
A time to grieve and a time to dance.

Ecclesiastes 3:4

I will comfort you there as a child
is comforted by its mother.

Isaiah 66:13

He heals the brokenhearted,
binding up their wounds.

Psalm 147:3

The grass withers, and the flowers fade,
but the word of God stands forever.

Isaiah 40:8

### A bedside thought

Believe this: Jesus, our Lord, the Perfect Son of God, felt all that we feel today. He felt great suffering and He knew what must happen to himself so that we could be free. He understands what hurts you today. Allow His love to cover the pain with just a little faith.

Just a little faith is all you need.

When your faith is tested, your endurance
has a chance to grow…
For when your endurance
is fully developed,
you will be strong in character
and ready for anything.

James 1:3-4

Those who plant in tears
will harvest with shouts of joy!
They weep as they go
to plant their seed,
but they sing
as they return with the harvest.

Psalm 126:5-6

Since he himself
has gone through suffering
and temptation,
he is able to help us
when we are being tempted.

Hebrews 2:18

# God is a Wonder!

## *Wonder in His Song*

## A bedside thought

Oh, how great is our God. Don't be nervous. Just praise Him like you know you belong to Him. That's right. We need to act like we belong to Him.  Somebody needs to hear your praise story. Somebody needs your song. Can you step out of your comfort zone and tell somebody how good the Lord has been to you and that He is a Way Maker? Can you lead the choir of your family with a song that will encourage somebody to 'Have a little talk with Jesus' to make it right?  Can you warm up your prayer life enough to remind yourself that He has promised never to leave you alone? Can you tell someone who is in her sleepless night that all she needs to do is 'Lean on the Everlasting Arms?' God will bless you for telling His story of Wonder.

# God Will Take Care of You

by Fanny Crosby

God will take care of you, be not afraid;
He is your safeguard through sunshine and shade;
Tenderly watching and keeping His own,
He will not leave you to wander alone.

God will take care of you, through all the day,
Shielding your footsteps, directing your way;
He is your shepherd, protector, and guide,
Leading His children where still waters glide.

God will take care of you long as you live,
Granting you blessings no other can give;

He will take care of you when time is past,
Safe to His kingdom will bring you at last.

God will take care of you still to the end;
Oh, what a Father, Redeemer, and Friend!

41

Jesus will answer whenever you call;
He will take care of you, trust Him for all.

### O Wonderful Savior

by E. F. Miller

I have heard a most wonderful story
Of Jesus, the Savior and King;
How He came from the bright realms of glory
Glad news of salvation to bring.

With the poor and the lowly He mingled-
Yes, even the vilest of men,
Showing mercy and love as they lingered,
To hear His blest words unto them.

A poor woman was brought to Him helpless,
To be stoned for her sins in the past;
He replied to them, "He that is sinless,
By him let the first stone be cast."

O wonderful, wonderful Savior,
Thy praises with joy we will sing:

For coming on earth to redeem us
We crown Thee forever our King!

## Oh, Wondrous Name

by Victoria Frances

Oh, wondrous Name, by prophets heard
Long years before His birth;
They saw Him coming from afar,
The Prince of Peace on earth.

Oh, glorious Name, the angels praise,
And ransomed saints adore,-
The Name above all other names,
Our refuge evermore.

Oh, precious Name, exalted high,
To Him all pow'r is giv'n;
Through Him we triumph over sin,
By Him we enter Heav'n.

The Wonderful! The Counselor!
The Great and Mighty Lord!
The everlasting Prince of Peace!
The King, the Son of God...

43

Do you have a special song about God?
One that holds you and refreshes your spirit?
List the words. Hum the tune.
His message of wonder and love will soothe you.

**Amazing Grace**

by John Newton

Amazing Grace, how sweet the sound,
That saved a wretch like me.
I once was lost but now am found,
Was blind, but now I see.

T'was Grace that taught my heart to fear.
And Grace, my fears relieved.
How precious did that Grace appear
The hour I first believed.

Through many dangers, toils and snares
I have already come;
'Tis Grace that brought me safe thus far
and Grace will lead me home…

## Blessed Assurance

by Fanny J. Crosby

Blessed assurance, Jesus is mine!
Oh, what a foretaste of glory divine!
Heir of salvation, purchase of God,
Born of His Spirit, washed in His blood.

Perfect submission, perfect delight,
Visions of rapture now burst on my sight;
Angels descending, bring from a above
Echoes of mercy, whispers of love.

Perfect submission, all is at rest,
I in my Saviour am happy and blest;
Watching and waiting, looking above,
Filled with His goodness, lost in His love.

This is my story, this is my song,
Praising my Saviour all the day long;
This is my story, this is my song,
Praising my Saviour all the day long

### I Will Give You Rest

by Catherine Harbison Waterman Eslingt

Come unto me, when shadows darkly gather,
When the sad heart is weary and distrest,
Seeking for comfort from your Heavenly Father,
Come unto me, and I will give you rest!

Ye who have mourned when the spring-flowers were taken,
When the ripe fruit fell richly to the ground,
When the loved slept, in brighter homes to waken,
Where their pale brows with spirit-wreaths are crowned;>/p>

Large are the mansions in thy Father's dwelling,
Glad are the homes that sorrows never dim;
Sweet are the harps in holy music swelling,
Soft are the tones which raise the heavenly hymn;

There, like an Eden blossoming in gladness,
Bloom the fair flowers the earth too rudely pressed;
Come unto me, all ye who droop in sadness,
Come unto me, and I will give you rest.

47

### A bedside thought

We can be so impatient sometimes. We actually run *in front* of God sometimes. How are we going to hear Him, walk with Him and be guided by His spirit of wonder if we try to do it all on our own? Let's get still in the waiting room and be encouraged and nourished by the matchless word of God. A song can sooth the way to calm.

### Resting on My Saviour's Love

by Eliza E. Hewitt

My heart is sweetly resting
Upon my Saviour's love,
Upon the grace that saves me,
For mansions bright above.

Afar I need not seek him,
He dwells within my soul,
And from the living fountains
Rich waves of blessing roll.

The more I lean upon him,
The more I learn his power,
And find his grace sufficient,
To meet life's every hour.

Resting, resting,
Resting on my Saviour's love,
Resting, resting,
On my Saviour's love

49

Your own story may become your own song!

God will hear your song of praise so clearly.

This time is just for you and God...

# God is a Wonder!

## *Wonder in*

## *His Comforting Arms*

**Loss, pain, depression or stress,**
**or even a shift in the atmosphere**
**can bring about discouraging feelings**
**that can overwhelm our days... and our nights.**
Sometimes we think it just will never happen
or maybe just never happen to us.
Each of our mountains and valleys are so uniquely different.

## It's all personal.

Grieving is personal.
Pain is personal.
Depression is personal.
Addiction is personal.
Loneliness is personal
Sickness is personal.
Love is personal.
Anger is personal.
Fear is personal.
Confusion is personal.
Your relationships are personal.
Stress is personal.
Your tears are personal.

Yet, there is One who understands every challenging life event.

God. The One Who made you ...and 'makes over' you.

There is One who hears your inner cry, anger, and confusion.

Our responses to those overwhelming feelings
are as individual as the hairs on our head
and the air each one of us breathes each day.

Because God is a wonder,
He can comfort you and give you His peace.

You are not alone.

The God of wonder is with you...right now.  Just call out His name.

He will recognize your voice, even if it's silent right now.
Even if you can't speak. Even if you're upset.
He knows your heart.

53

## A bedside thought

"Lord, can you stop the <u>CHAOS</u> in my MIND?  Please?"

The mind is a wonderful creation. You know how it feels when you are in congested traffic. Most folk don't care for traffic.  In big cities it might be a passionate experience and yelling for a taxi, the norm. That justifies street traffic. Think about the clutter of 'traffic' that is in our mind.  At times we just can't free up our minds. Some traffic can become programmed in our minds: "You will never be anything! You will not succeed! You will never be good enough!" You can't love or be loved." SUCH UNTRUTH!  WITH GOD ALL THINGS ARE POSSIBLE (Matthew 19:26). We beat ourselves up every day. We don't forgive ourselves. We engage in forgetfulness about what God has done, or the grace that we have been given. Unknowingly. through the war.  Then...you remember! You can go straight to the Saviour...for the ultimate rescue. We struggle with world issues and what the world promises.  You may call out to God, but He seems be so distant from you and your circumstances.  Self-talk or book of affirmations don't work,  but there is always God. If we remember His promises for you and for me, the view becomes clearer.  You see, God can <u>clear out the chaos</u>.

God understands and is sensitive to your life circumstances.
The bible has shown us individuals who had challenging
life events that troubled them day and night.  There were many
depressed, troubled folk in the bible.  Many of them
had days and nights like ours.  King David was deeply troubled by fear.
Elijah spent many a night, discouraged.  Job was devastated
with great loss and physical illness. Moses grieved over the sin
of his people. Jeremiah felt insecure and lonely.
Peter struggled about denying Jesus.  Jesus, our Lord
felt ALL that we feel today. He felt great suffering and
He knew what must happen to himself so that we could be free.


God is a wonder because He 'checks in' on those

who need a Saviour.

"Before they call, I will answer;

while they are still speaking, I will hear."

(Isaiah 65:24)

55

# A bedside thought

## Pain

Somebody today is really hurting inside.

The enemy wants us 'tore up from the floor up'. He wants us defeated and depleted. We have so many internal wars with ourselves. We lose energy, we can't concentrate, and we don't eat right or sleep right. Life situations can discourage us so much, we feel hopeless. Some say we need to have spiritual renewal classes. An adult coloring book might be calming until the phone rings, but it won't provide the everlasting peace of Someone I know. We need more than an O-M-G every time something or someone surprises, denies or revises our plan in life. We need a Savior who can comfort us. The Word of God has some statistics for the troubled times in lives of plain folk like you and I, and The Word of God's solution is in perfect harmony.

The Book of Psalms, Chapter 77 shares the story of Asaph,
a servant of God who was stressed, depressed
and had many restless nights.
We really don't know the fine-tuned details
of Asaph's restless nights. That's okay.
Everybody doesn't need to know
all the details of your restless nights.
Go to God first,
and He will bring those individuals to your atmosphere
that will bless you.
Asaph was persistent.  He went straight to our Father.
He didn't consume the burden on a friend at this point.
He didn't attempt to dry his sorrows in a bottle.
He didn't turn up with his so-called associates.
He didn't complain to his employer.
He called on the Lord…directly.

Isn't it wonderful,
to not have to have anyone's permission
to inhale the presence of God?
Yes, you can talk to the Father, right now…

## A bedside thought

Encourage yourself.

About 20 years ago, I heard a minister say that a lot of people contact him and ask the all familiar request, "Please pray for me". He told his congregation that sometimes we just need to go straight to God with our requests. Depending on God alone is priceless. Humans do error. Even those who love us. Don't get mad if one of your friends or family member doesn't have all the answers. Don't be upset because someone doesn't have the right words to ease your spirit. They are very human. Give it to God. Yes, give it to God. Get still, wherever you are, and tell your Creator EVERYTHING. Don't forget to be patient for His response.

**Guess what?**

**God loves you.
You don't have to believe me.
His Word is full of His promises
of love...**

### A bedside thought

Asaph (Psalm 77) was a participant in a true cry-out to God, to the point of exhaustion. We know God, but we can feel like we are in a distant land. Meditation at this point can be chaotic and abstract, and disoriented. Can you take a minute or two to just think about God. I mean, really - just God. Oh, take some time to consider His wonder. Take some time to just be in His glory. His peace. His love. Don't sway...stay there, with Him.

Our Lord knows all about being human.
Our Lord Jesus, in his humanness, was in distress.
With His precious hands
stretched out with nails driven them.
Jesus knew about pain. I know we have heard the words,
"I called on the Lord, and He heard my cry and
joy comes in the morning". But nights *sur*e can be long.
The light of heaven is not always in view.
Our focused prayers may become foggy and unfocused.
Sometimes we can be paralyzed  - not just physically,
but mentally and emotionally paralyzed. Yes, paralyzed.
With no rest. Sleepless and speechless.
The National Institutes of Health state that the first sign of
clinical depression is a lack of sleep.  Have you had any
good sleep lately? Sometimes the God that we know and believe in,
must slow us down so we can hear him.
Now, you can rest and get refreshed to feel the warm love of God.

Think only about yourself for
a few minutes. Just you.
It's okay.
It's better than okay.

Relax, Inhale and Exhale.

Get in a **relaxing** position if you can.
Begin to think of feeling comfortable. Take your time.
Think of something good that has happened in your life. **Inhale.**
Just one thing? Or maybe more than one thing. If not, a hope.
Thank your Creator for that. **Exhale.** Was it an event?
Was it a storm that you thought wouldn't calm?
**Inhale** the Goodness of God. Remember all that
He has done and for Who He is. **Exhale.**
Commune on the thought that His Word states
that all things work for us. **Inhale** this promise: And we know that
in "all things God works for the good of those who love him,
who have been called according to his purpose". (Roman 8:28)
**Exhale.** Think for a minute and reflect on that.
All things…those things you thought were impossible to get through,
all things…those struggles that keeps pinching you, all things…that issue
that you feel you can't tell anyone about.
**Inhale.**
Commune with prayer in conversation and fresh relationship with your Lord.
**Exhale** the praise.
I know, it may not feel like things are working in your favor at this moment.
But God is faithful and desires you to know that He is working on your behalf
even now. You can trust Him. **Inhale** a little faith.
Create mental photo book of things that you got through. Give a little thanks.
It takes just a little faith to feel His glory. **Exhale** more praise.
Thank you, Lord, for getting me through that.
Thank you, Lord, for getting someone I care for through that event.

# God is a Wonder!

## *Wonder in His Forgiveness*

My dear friend, there is a journey to peace through forgiveness.
Oh, how we crave peace even when we don't know it.

Knowing that God will forgive you grants peace.
Forgiving others grants peace.
Forgiving yourself grants peace.
And accepting forgiveness - truly grants peace.
**God will forgive you.**
Feeling guilty is real, too. No matter how much we hurt.
God will ease the hurt.

"Your heavenly Father will forgive you if you forgive
those who sin against you.' (Matthew 6:14)
God will forgive you, and repenting means you really want to
try not to repeat the sin. Just commit and He will assist you.
It is a refreshing sunburst of His love. It frees you. Don't you want
to rest better and feel true freedom? Forgiveness begins that journey.

If we confess our sins, he is faithful and just to forgive
us our sins and to cleanse us from all unrighteousness.

### Meditate on His perfect and true Word:

*"I alone am he who blots away your sins for my own sake and will never think of them again". (Isaiah 43:25)*

### Repenting is real. Trusting God's promises is real.

When you learn to ask God for forgiveness, realize that He
is giving you a great lesson and opportunity to
get comfortable
and set free by asking others to forgive you.
Now if they don't respond. It's okay. You did your part.
Just be sincere.
If they don't accept your apology, again,
you did your part. Just be sincere.
God will handle the rest.

### Forgive others.
Even that person that said, ....??
Yes. Forgive others. I'm the first in line of having rough times.
Many have experienced devastating circumstances
and mountains we have not been equipped to climb,
and valleys so low we begin to lose all hope.
Sometimes everything we want to live for, we live against.

We trespass against those we trespass,
we are disobedient to God's will, we suffer the unbelievable,

we refuse to forgive and sometimes
we just won't even forgive ourselves.
And we do this while knowing God.

### Do you need to forgive someone?

Have you been waiting 15 years for someone to say
"I'm sorry" to you?  What does "I'm sorry" really mean?
Look at what the God of Wonder's instruction says about forgiveness.
His Word has eternal benefits:

"Hate stirs up trouble, but love forgives all offenses."
(Proverbs 10:12)

"Forgive someone, and you will strengthen your friendship.
Keep reminding them, and you will destroy it." (Proverbs 17.9)

### Question of the day:
### Are you mad at God?
### Something really, really didn't go your way?

Did it really hurt you or someone you love?  Loved?

God does not have thin skin.  God understands every emotion
and reaction and response that you could ever act upon.
God is sovereign. He is in control and in full authority
of all things. He has all power and He is the creator
of love and forgiveness. Begin a trust in Him.
Begin with the promises of His Word related to forgiveness.

*Tell Him all about your situation and your feelings.*
*Yell back His promises to Him.*

*He hears you.*
*He feels your tears.*
*He understands what you don't understand.*
*Go ahead, talk to Him: "Lord you promised….*
*And Lord, you promised in your Word."*

Surely the arm of the Lord is not too short to save, nor his ear too dull. (2 Chronicles 7:14) says" If my people, who are called by my name, will humble themselves and pray
and seek my face
(Cry if you must!)
and turn from their wicked ways,
then will I hear from heaven and will forgive their sin
and will heal their land."
**Forgive yourself.**

**Forgive yourself.**

**Forgive yourself.**

"Some of the most miserable people are those who don't forgive themselves." (Psalms 51:1-3)

God is Generous in love – God, give me grace!

God is Huge in mercy- wipe out my bad record!

Lord, scrub away my guilt, soak out my sins in your laundry!

I know how bad I've been; my sins are staring me down!

1. Will the Lord reject forever?
2. Will he never show his favor again?
3. Has his unfailing love vanished forever?
4. Has his promise failed for all time?

God IS a wonder. Trust Him to forgive you.

Trust Him to help you forgive yourself.

# God is a Wonder!

## *Wonder at His Altar Call*

# Taking it all to the altar

Growing up in a small Baptist church,
there was always a time in the service
where the pastor commenced an altar call
where members walked to the front altar
and he would offer a communal prayer.
Today there is a choice of staying just where you are
and still engaging in prayer.
This is what is so special about our Wonderful God.
Wherever you are right now,
you can take everything to the altar. All your challenges,
your fears. All your tears.
Even if you just want to thank Him,
you can do it from right where you are.
Morning, noon or night.
And, yes, even in the middle of the night,
He is here for you. God is a wonder.
Let the conversations begin. Trust God, He is listening.

Even if it's your first prayer, He will hear you.
Even if you don't speak it or write it.
He is so awesome. He knows what you desire.
He knows your thoughts and your tears.

Is your all at the altar?

# Is Your All on The Altar

*by Elisha A. Hoffman*

You have longed for sweet peace,
and for faith to increase,
And have earnestly fervently pray'd;
But you cannot have rest, or be perfectly blest
Until all on the altar is laid.
Would you walk with the Lord,
in the light of His Word?
And have peace and contentment always,
You must do His sweet will, to be free from all ill,
On the altar your all you must lay.
Is your all on the altar of sacrifice laid?
Your heart, does the Spirit control?
You can only be blest and have peace and sweet rest,
As you yield Him your body and soul.
Oh, we never can know what the Lord will bestow
Of the blessings for which we have pray'd.
Til our body and soul He doth fully control,

*And our all on the altar is laid.*
*Who can tell all the love He will send from above?*
*And how happy our hearts will be made,*
*Of the fellowship sweet we shall share at His feet,*
*When our all on the altar is laid.*
*Is your all on the altar of sacrifice laid?*
*Your heart, does the Spirit control?*
*You can only be blest and have peace and sweet rest,*
*As you yield Him your body and soul*

**You can begin to share your
deepest thoughts with the Perfect Listener:**

*Oh, Lord, teach me how to pray…*

*Hear my prayers, Oh Lord of All*

*Your plans just for me!*

*My prayer at the altar:*

75

*Can we talk Lord?*

### A bedside thought

Talking it out - can literally heal us and bless our souls. Our despair cannot only affect our own body, mind and spirit but others around us. But see, out of our chaos, God and only God can bring order, love and peace, and joy. Now is the time that you can depend on Him - the Author and Finisher of love. God will never, never leave us or forsake us. Christ had an awesome resurrection and you and I have grace from the living Jesus. Tell Him boldly about you and your concerns. Talking to the Saviour will build your friendship. You can trust Him. That's called faith.

78

*I am going to trust you, Lord.*

*You have no equal, Lord.*

80

*Your wonders are with no limit!*

## A bedside thought

Have you stopped praying? Are you feeling legitimately angry as you deal with unbearable life experiences? The God of Wonder can give you His peace. Inhale. Exhale. Have a talk to the Saviour. Take your time. Do what you can. He will handle the rest. See, God never leaves. We leave Him. BELIEVE THIS: "AND WE KNOW THAT IN ALL THINGS GOD WORKS FOR THE GOOD OF THOSE WHO LOVE HIM, WHO HAVE BEEN CALLED ACCORDING TO HIS PURPOSE" (Romans 8:28). Let's continue the Lord's understanding in The Message translation: "Meanwhile, the moment we get tired in the waiting, God's Spirit is right alongside helping us along. If we don't know how or what to pray, it doesn't matter. He does our praying for us, making prayer out of our wordless sighs, and our aching groans. He knows us far better than we know ourselves. He knows our present condition and keeps us present before God. That's why we can be so sure that every detail in our lives of love for God is worked into something good" (Romans 8:26-28).

Our God, Our God...is a wonder!

83

*Your Word, O Lord, is eternal*

85

86

*You told me to 'be still" ...here I am, Lord.*

88

*I know you GOT THIS ONE GOD!*

# God is a Wonder!

## *Wonder in*

## *His Gift of Salvation*

**O LORD my God,
you have performed many wonders for us.
Your plans for us are too numerous to list.
You have no equal.**

He offers His mercy and grace and we don't even deserve it.

But he continues to bless us anyway.

"God so loved the world that He gave His only begotten son

that whosoever believes in Him shall not perish

but have everlasting life."

(John 3:16)

"Our Father who art in Heaven,
Hallowed be Thy Name.
Thy Kingdom come, Thy Will be done,
On earth as it is in Heaven.
Give us this day our daily bread,
And forgive us our trespasses (debts) as we

forgive those who trespass against us

(our debtors).
And lead us not into temptation,

but deliver us from evil.
For thine is the Kingdom and the

Power and the Glory forever. Amen."

(Matthew 6:9-13)

A listening ear is available to you...

The risen Jesus said: "Listen! I am standing at the door,

knocking; if you hear my voice and open the door,

I will come into you". (Rev 3:20)

Loving grace is available to you...


"By grace you have been saved through faith;

and that not of yourselves, it is the gift of God;

not as a result of works,

that no one should boast". (Ephesians 2:8,9)

### *I BELIEVE by Gwendolyn Hayes*

*I believe…*

*God is God.*

*He is the One who has not been created.*

*He is the awesome creator of this world!*

*He is all knowing and all loving.*

*I love Him because He first loved me.*

*He loved me even before my mother called out my name.*

*He awesomely designed*

*and birthed Jesus the Christ as the son of God.*

*He is the reason for grace and mercy!*

*How many paths of young men and women will I cross today?*

*Will I leave some of God's love, grace and mercy with them?*

*I believe that Jesus following the law of His Father, died on the Cross,*

*at Calvary for my sins and yours.*

*I believe His last breath was our first breath of Love.*

*I know as He rose on the third day, He washed away my*

*sins and made me free.*

*I know that all I do is through His strength!*

*I truly believe that the Bible is the complete and wonderfully*

*inspired Word of God.*

*I believe that my God gave us the Holy Spirit*

*to hold and love us here on earth.*

*I believe in all eternity and eternal praise to the Father.*

**What do you believe today?**

You are cordially invited to have your best

**bedside inspiration** and **nourishment** for **your** spirit each day.

Do you want to get to know the God of Wonder?

Do you want to become even closer in your relationship with Him?

God gives us grace and mercy <u>every day</u>.

God gives us grace and mercy <u>every night.</u>

What an opportunity to refresh our spirits with His love.

**God** is a wonder. **God** is love.

## A bedside thought

You could be the one who cries out to some -thing.  Or you might think you are indestructible and lean to your own understanding or take the advice of those who are as much in the dark as you are. If you live long enough you may have a time or two or three, when you thought you were going to lose your complete mind.  If you live long enough, you might wonder what or who you should really put your trust in. All the world has to offer are a few temporary tranquilizers to calm your mood.  The world has no answers, not a clue. We were purchased for a price. That price was purchased with the life of Jesus.  What if it was you or me?  Being dragged through town and beat and stabbed and nailed up on a cross for all for sinners. Wouldn't you like to get to know the One who was purchased for you and me?  Wouldn't you like to get to know the One you can trust and depend on?  Say YES! Or even Say YES, AGAIN! The God of WONDER offers you the opportunity to be in His love story today.

### John 3:16 says:

For God so loved the world, that he gave his only begotten
son that whosoever believeth in Him shall have everlasting life.

### John 3:16 The Message Translation says:

16-18 "This is how much God loved the world: He gave his Son, his one and only
Son. And this is why: so that no one need be destroyed; by believing in him,
anyone can have a whole and lasting life. But God didn't go to all the trouble of
sending his Son merely to point an accusing finger, telling the world how bad it
was. He came to help, to put the world right again. Anyone who trusts in him is
acquitted; anyone who refuses to trust him has long since been under the death
sentence without knowing it. And why? Because of that person's failure to believe
in the one-of-a-kind Son of God when introduced to him.

### Juan 3:16 Spanish says:

Porque de tal manera amó Dios al mundo, que ha dado á su Hijo unigénito, para
que todo aquel que en él cree, no se pierda, mas tenga vida eterna.

**यूहत्रा** 3:16 Nepali says:

16 हो, परमेश्वरले संसारलाई यति साहो प्रेम गर्नुभयो, कि उहाँले आफ्ना एकमात्र पुत्रलाई दिनु भयो। परमेश्वरले आफ्ना पुत्रलाई दिनु भयो त्यस द्वारा उहाँमाथि विश्वास गर्ने कोहीपनि नाश हुने छैन, तर अनन्त जीवन प्राप्त गर्नेछ।

**요한복음** 3:16 Korean says:

"하나님이 세상을 무척 사랑하셔서 하나밖에 없는 외아들마저 보내 주셨으니 누구든지 그를 믿기만 하면 멸망하지 않고 영원한 생명을 얻는다.

## American Sign Language Translation for John 3:16

https://youtu.be./WusDXuqXxH0

# This is <u>your</u> invitation

## to God's gift of salvation!

**The 'whosever' is you!** The Creator of the best Word,
the best Song,  the One who gives the best Comfort, and the One
to have the best Altar call relationship with, offers **YOU**
His gift of love.  God **IS** a wonder! He takes care of all things.
He wipes away the tears, no more sorrow, death or pain –
away with all those reminders, unwanted memories.
Would you nourish your spirit by accepting Him
as your personal Savior? Your God of Wonder?
No matter where I am in my life, **LORD OF ALL**...
your promises are real and available to me!


I hear music in the air, there must a **God** somewhere...

100

In His wonder, **God** has made us overcomers!
If you would like to accept
Jesus Christ
as **your** personal and eternal Saviour,
make this a new altar space with your name attached:


**Dear God**, I want to know you, I want to know what
plans and songs you have for me for my life. I have read for
myself, and believe that you sent your precious and
Only son Jesus Christ to die on the cross to save the world. You sent Him to
save sinners. And that includes me. I am asking your forgiveness of my sins
including those I don't even know I
have committed. I accept you as my personal Savior. I need you.
*Thank you for your faithfulness, your love and your wonder.*

In Jesus' name, Amen


**Your name:** _____

**Write this wonderful date down right here:** _____

Blessings are yours forever!

You will find true peace in the **Holy One.**


**Your eternal gift of salvation is from God,**

**because God is a Wonder!**

May our good Lord continue to bless you!

"I waited patiently for the Lord and He turned to me

and heard my cry." (Psalms 40:1)

**and He will always nourish your spirit,**

**because God is a Wonder!**

**GOD IS A WONDER!**

*My personal thoughts about my salvation:*

*God*
*is*
*a*
*wonder!*

## *Gwendolyn's special' Thank-you Café'*

*Thank you to my daughter-in-law Tanya,*
*for your everyday fresh spirit of love; my mother-in-law,*
*Taliba (Lady Moms) for your priceless family prayers;*
*my son Millon, my husband Ephrem, my sister Joylyn,*
*my niece Jada; and of course,*
*my sisterfriends Dr. Lillie, Vicki, Saundra, and Thelma*
*for listening to me, praying for me,*
*and hearing the 'stuff in my brain',*
*and still cheering me on.*
*To First Lady, Rev. Deborah Pounds & Pastor Roderick Pound, Sr.*
*for allowing me to serve the women and congregation of our church.*
*Thank you to church and family friends:*
*Deacon George and Deaconess Vickie Hogan,*
*Deacon Jeff and Deaconess Tina Foreman, and*
*Deacon Jim and Deaconess Cyndy Whitfield,*
*and Pianist Eda Mae Prisby*
*as I continue to observe your priceless servant love.*

**You are all the sugar and milk in my tea,**
**and MY bursts of sunshine!**

## Spiritual Notes

https://www.biblegateway.com

Bible scriptures: The Holy Bible, King James Version

Bible scriptures: The Holy Bible, New International Version

Bible scriptures: The Holy Bible, The Message Translation

Bible scriptures: The Holy Bible, Spanish Version

Bible scriptures: The Holy Bible, Chinese Version

Bible scriptures: The Holy Bible, Nepali Translation

Translation for the deaf: https://youtu.be./WusDXuqXxH0

Public Domain Lyrics from the following:

Hymnary.org., Timeless Truths.org, www.pdinfo.com

* The author chooses to use the Name/spelling "Saviour"
and the Name/spelling "Savior" in this project as appropriate.

**God is a Wonder:**
Bedside inspirations to nourish your spirit
**Your Sun is Coming!  Sunbursts of Conversation Guide**

This section is offered for your continued conversations, bible study
or to encourage yourself even more!
Take your time, choose your way to commune.

## 1.  God is a Wonder!  Wonder in His Word

I Peter 2:2) says that we should be "like newborn babies,
long for the pure milk of the word, so that by it you may grow in respect
and salvation." Let God's word be first. Let God's word speak to your spirit first.
It will nourish you first. No better guide for direction as (Psalm 119:105).
"Your word is a lamp to guide me and a light for my path."

We can surely encourage ourselves as we daily keep
God's word within for daily growth. Do you have some bible verses that you
know can calm and refresh your spirit as soon as you think or recite of them?

His Word is eternal. It doesn't change like the world's rules, policies and
commitments.

Inhale the God of Wonder's message of love and then share it.

Oh, you won't be able to keep the Word to yourself but,
do keep the Word in your heart.

## 2. God is a Wonder! Wonder in His Song

Each song is a story. Each song is a soothing testimony. (James 5:13) says," if one is suffering, they should pray and if cheerful sing praise".

Music is a wonderful way to get some praise and worship in your day. God loves our worship and praise through song." Like David we can sing dance and celebrate His wonder. Even if you are thinking about it or not as mobile as you once were, God feels your gratitude!

How will you celebrate God even in a storm or restless night? Can you praise Him through the storm?

Oh, there is a song just for you
It will appear. Just ask the Savior will hold you and comfort your spirit today and always.

## 3. God is a Wonder! Wonder in His Comforting Arms

God does hear our cries in (Psalm 77:1-20). Think about the Musician, Asaph who" cried out to God".

He took some time to get still, and think
about the snapshots of God's presence in the past, and that refreshed him
to look to the future. When there are dark, depressing, anxious times

when hope feels like it is nowhere in sight, God is still God. He will comfort you when you need Him most. He has the answers that no man has.

*God has a way of reminding of His love and commitment to us.*

*Your memories will comfort you. And it can be an awesome time to begin watching*

*God can create memories for you.*

## 4. God is a Wonder! Wonder in His Forgiveness

Do you need to forgive someone? Have you been waiting 15 years to say 'I'm sorry' to someone? God has eternal benefits for forgiveness. Unforgiveness can be a sad and lonely feeling. God will forgive you just for asking.

**I John 1:9 says, "But if we confess our sings to him, he is faithful and just to forgive us our sins and to cleanse us from all wickedness". Also, "If you forgive others who have sinned against you, your heavenly Father will for give you. But if you refuse to forgive others, your Father will not forgive your sins". (Matthew 6:14-15).**

What could be worse than God being unforgiving?

## 5.  God is a Wonder! Wonder in His Altar Call

God is a prayer answering God! Jesus is on the mainline,
tell Him what you want.
Call Him up and tell Him what you want (A Spiritual).

The awesome thing about talking with God, is that He hears everything
that you take to Him sincerely. **(I John 5:14) tells us
"This is the confidence we have in approaching God: that if
we ask anything according to his will, he hears us.** No need for a
performance to please humans. A simple chat works fine for God.


Yet, can we begin by giving thanks to the Creator of the world for
just being God. For looking out for you. For the sun and the rain. For love.
For safety. For peace. For the people who are keeping you in
prayer right now. Giving thanks is as easy as asking for something. God first.
Do you think praying for yourself is selfish? Not at all.
Take everything to God. Can you look to God first, before anyone else? He
desires this in His word: **"Look to the Lord and his strength; see his face
always." (2 Chronicles 6:21)** He will even give you strength to take another's
burden to Him. Can you consider taking another's burden to the altar?

### 6. God is a Wonder! Wonder in His Gift of Salvation

Salvation is a gift. Don't you like gifts! **(Ephesians 2:8) tells us "For by grace you have been saved through faith; and that not of yourselves, it is the gift of God."** Salvation is eternal. You with God because of His grace.

There is only One that can rescue us from our circumstances. How do we thank Him? We thank Him for His grace. We give glory to God with our faith, even if it starts off being just a little bit. He knows your heart. He really does. He created it.

What a wonderful connection you have with the Creator of the world.  It's so good, again - we can't keep it to ourselves. Share the story of the God of Wonder with another!

No formal certifications need. Just an honest heart of love for God is all that is needed
.
He loved you first, so how are you going to show your gratitude today and each day following today?

## The Author: Gwendolyn Hayes

is a licensed minister and a women's ministry class facilitator at Second Baptist Church of Akron, Ohio. Gwendolyn is a regional conference speaker, trainer and consultant for non-profits. She is the founder and CEO of Gwendolyn Hayes Clear View Consulting, LLC and Dandelion Dreams, Inc. Gwendolyn is the author of Mrs. Bumblebee and Her Counting Wings, Mrs. Bumblebee and Her Perfectly Perfect Nature Friends, artist/producer for the CD, When He Touched Me and producer for this project's accompanying CD, Your Sun is Coming: A Piano and Drum session to nourish your spirit! She is the designer for the Praying Angel Pillows and the founder of Your Sun is Coming conferences. Gwendolyn received a Bachelor of Science and Master of Education from Kent State University, a Christian Education certification from Ashland University, and an Education Specialist degree at Northcentral University. She is currently completing a Doctor of Education focused on church leadership. Gwendolyn has served on board of the American Cancer Society and as a former chaplain for Zeta Phi Beta Sorority, Inc. Gwendolyn has an extremely beautiful bouquet of children and grandchildren. Gwendolyn writes, worships, and plays in northeastern Ohio with her husband, traveling chef, spiritual poet, and favorite prayer partner, Minister Ephrem Hayes.

**For speaking engagements and book signings contact:**

**Gwendolyn Hayes:**

Website:  Gwendolynhayesclearviewconsulting.com

E-mail:  ghclearviewconsultingllc@gmail.com

Phone:  330-794-3163

**Leave your confidential prayer requests at:**

**wewillbeprayingforyou@gmail.com**

There's more....

'Your Sun is Coming' Women Conference
Check soon for an upcoming event near you!
at
http://gwendolynhayesclearviewconsulting.com


Your Sun is Coming – Tee shirts!

Your Sun is Coming: Piano & Drumming CD
Accompany CD for this Project!

Praying Angel Pillows for everyone!

Study Well Pillows and Totes for students of all ages!

# Notes

# Notes

# Notes